SMOKING
A RISKY BUSINESS

SMOKING
A RISKY BUSINESS

LAURENCE PRINGLE

MORROW JUNIOR BOOKS • NEW YORK

The author thanks Karen H. Lewis, Assistant Director,
Tobacco Policy Projects, The Advocacy Institute, for reading
the manuscript of this book and helping to improve its accuracy.

Cartoons on pp. 67 and 88: Doonesbury © 1996, 1995 G. B. Trudeau. Reprinted with permission of Universal Press Syndicate. All rights reserved.

Permission for the following photographs is gratefully acknowledged: American Cancer Society, pp. 2, 26, 39, 43, 49, 53, 78, 84; AP/Wide World Photos, pp. 69, 105; Coalition on Smoking OR Health, p. 98; Minnesota Department of Health, pp. 41, 108; New York Public Library Picture Collection, pp. 12, 14, 15, 16; Richard Pollay, Curator, History of Advertising Archives, University of British Columbia, pp. 34–35; Sean Pringle, p. 46; Stop Teenage Addiction to Tobacco, p. 96; U.S. Department of Agriculture, pp. 18, 28, 60, 101. All other photographs by the author.

Copyright © 1996 by Laurence Pringle

Designed by Trish Parcell Watts.
Printed in the United States of America.

1 2 3 4 5 6 7 8 9 10

Library of Congress Cataloging-in-Publication Data
Pringle, Laurence P.
Smoking: a risky business/Laurence Pringle.
p. cm.
Includes bibliographical references and index.
Summary: Provides a history of tobacco products and smoking, with a discussion of harmful effects and changing social attitudes.
ISBN 0-688-13039-9
1. Tobacco habit—United States—Juvenile literature. 2. Cigarette habit—United States—Juvenile literature. 3. Smoking—United States—Juvenile literature. 4. Tobacco—United States—Physiological effect—Juvenile literature. 5. Tobacco industry—United States—Juvenile literature. [1. Tobacco habit. 2. Smoking.] I. Title. HV5760.P75 1996 362.29'6—dc20 96-5359 CIP AC

CONTENTS

SMOKING

A RISKY BUSINESS

INTRODUCTION

In 1604, King James of England wrote that smoking was "a custom lothsome to the eye, hatefull to the Nose, harmefull to the braine, dangerous to the Lungs...."

His *Counterblaste to Tobacco* was issued at a time when many believed that tobacco smoke helped fight disease. Men, women, and even children were urged to inhale tobacco smoke to ward off the deadly plague. In 1603 an English boy wrote of the harsh whipping he received one morning—his punishment for not smoking a pipe of tobacco as ordered by school authorities.

Nearly four centuries after King James's attack on tobacco, cigarette packages and advertisements include warnings similar to those of King James—with different spelling!—that smoking is harmful and dangerous. A great deal has been learned about the effects of tobacco use since the days of King James. Yet midway through the twentieth century medical doctors still prescribed smoking for health reasons, as a harmless way to help lose weight. And today spokespeople for the tobacco industry, as well as scientists employed by the industry, continue to claim that a direct link between tobacco and disease has not been proved.

The story of tobacco and smoking is complex. For millions of people, it is a story of personal pleasure, addiction, and, frequently, premature death. It is also a story of a highly profitable and powerful industry doing its best to thrive and expand. And it is a story of United States government agencies spending public funds to aid the tobacco industry at home and abroad, while other arms of the government work to help people stop smoking or encourage them to never start.

Tobacco has been called the only legally available product that when used as directed causes death. Most people, including most smokers, know this grim fact. Nevertheless, worldwide the number of smokers is growing, and young people continue to be lured into an addiction that may take their very lives.

The story of tobacco and smoking is fascinating. It involves vital issues of science and politics, and critical health choices for every person.

1 AMERICA'S "GIFT" TO THE WORLD

"If you can't send money, send tobacco."
—General George Washington,
in a 1776 letter to the Continental Congress

In 1492, Christopher Columbus explored Caribbean islands he had "discovered" and wrote about the customs of the Tainos people who lived there. The Indians, as he called them, brought many gifts, including "a kind of dry leaf that they hold in great esteem."

In early November of that year, two of Columbus's men observed Tainos men and women "carrying a charred hollow wood in their hand, and herbs to smoke in this wood, which they are in the habit of doing."

The highly esteemed leaves and the herb that was smoked were the same plant: tobacco. The Tainos inhaled tobacco smoke through their nostrils. Other native American groups rolled dry tobacco leaves into a tube shape, tied the leaves tight, lit them, and inhaled the smoke through their mouths. Others smoked tobacco in pipes

An 1820 painting of a Cree family illustrates that tobacco was an important part of Native American life.

made of clay, stone, or wood. Europeans had never before seen anyone "drink" smoke, as they called it.

More than sixty kinds of tobacco grow in North and South America, and nearly all Native American people used these plants long before 1492. However, since Columbus heard the Tainos name for a Caribbean variety of tobacco, today we call all species of these plants by that name: tobacco.

According to anthropologists, the earliest known image of

tobacco use is a carving found in a Mayan temple in southern Mexico. It shows smoke coming from a long pipe held by a man who may be a shaman—a priest or medicine man. The earliest uses of tobacco were mostly religious. Native Americans believed tobacco had magical powers—to give warriors courage, appease the gods, cure illness, ensure a good harvest or a successful hunt, and so on.

Christopher Columbus took some tobacco leaves back to Queen Isabella of Spain. English and Portuguese explorers also brought tobacco plants and seeds home. Early settlers in the New World and crew members of sailing ships were the first Europeans to try tobacco themselves. Whenever an officer ordered the sailors to stop, they found this difficult if not impossible to do.

By the mid-1500s, tobacco was being grown in England, France, Portugal, and Spain. The use of tobacco spread around the world—to Africa, India, China, and Japan.

Wherever people smoked tobacco—usually in pipes   the habit stirred controversy. Although there was no medical evidence in those times that tobacco was harmful, clergymen sensed correctly that it was a mind-altering drug. They often called the use of tobacco an evil vice.

Others, however, promoted it as medicine. In 1559, Jean Nicot, the French ambassador to Portugal, sent tobacco plants to friends at home and later urged people to use tobacco to treat wounds, and even to cure cancer. (The botanical name for tobacco plants, *Nicotiana,* is named after Jean Nicot. So is tobacco's best-known ingredient, nicotine.) Tobacco was also thought to be a possible cure for asthma, a disease of the respiratory system.

Tobacco leaves being unloaded from a wagon in the early 1800s, when tobacco was already a highly profitable crop in the South.

It was not until the late 1700s that most people gave up the notion that tobacco could cure disease. Meanwhile, some government leaders took drastic steps to discourage people from using tobacco. In 1633, Sultan Murad IV of Turkey believed that smoking reduced the fighting abilities of his soldiers, so he ordered tobacco users hanged, beheaded, or starved to death. About the same time in Russia, Czar Mikhail Fedorovich ordered that tobacco users be punished. Persistent users were killed. In 1683, a Chinese law declared that anyone possessing tobacco would be beheaded.

Nevertheless, tobacco use spread and increased. Spain dominated the tobacco market for more than two centuries, partly because its plantations grew an especially mild variety of tobacco.

English settlers in Virginia had poor results at first because the local variety of tobacco was harsh tasting. However, by about 1612 they managed to get tobacco seeds from one of Spain's colonies in the Caribbean. The seeds did well in Virginia soil, and new ways of drying the tobacco leaves improved their flavor. Tobacco soon became a major crop of the Virginia colony. The Spanish monopoly was broken.

The ways of using tobacco have changed through time. Beginning in the 1700s, the practice of smoking pipes went out of style in England. The fashionable way to take tobacco was to inhale powdered tobacco leaves—called snuff—into the nostrils. The cigarette—bits of tobacco leaves within a little tube of paper—became

Smoking tobacco in pipes was common until, thanks to automated cigarette-rolling machines, cigarettes became less expensive.

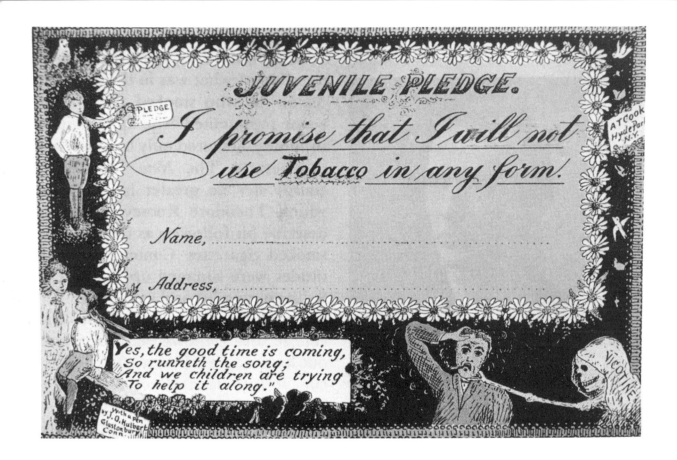

JUVENILE PLEDGE.

I promise that I will not use Tobacco in any form!

Name, ...

Address, ...

"Yes, the good time is coming,
So runneth the song;
And we children are trying
To help it along."

In the United States, pledge cards like this were given to children in schools and churches in the late 1800s and early 1900s, when public opposition to smoking reached an early peak.

popular in Europe during the mid-1800s. All cigarettes were rolled by hand, however, which added to their cost.

In 1880, a twenty-year-old Virginian named James Albert Bonsack applied for a patent on his invention: a cigarette-rolling machine. After some improvements, the steam-powered Bonsack machine did the work of forty-eight workers rolling cigarettes by hand. The cost of cigarettes dropped. Further changes in ways of curing tobacco leaves also improved the taste of cigarettes. The popularity of cigarettes grew, helped considerably by the invention early in the twentieth century of a safe kind of match. Until then, smokers had no safe, easily carried way of lighting up.

In the twentieth century, cigarettes mostly replaced pipes, cigars, snuff, and chewing tobacco as the favored way to use tobacco. And during this same time period it was learned that smoking cigarettes is the most dangerous way to use tobacco.

Nicotine is a poison within tobacco plants that defends them against leaf-eating insects.

2 NICOTINE: A MIND-ALTERING DRUG

"Heroin addicts say it is easier to give up dope than it is to give up smoking."

—Dr. Sharon Hall
University of California Medical Center, San Francisco

Bartholomé de Las Casas accompanied Christopher Columbus on voyages to the Caribbean in 1498 and 1502. He wrote of "paper firecrackers" called "tobaccos" that were smoked by the natives and by Spanish settlers, "who, after I reprimanded them, saying it was a vice, answered that they were unable to stop taking it."

Today, nearly a billion people on earth smoke cigarettes. Many have tried to stop, and they, too, find that smoking can be extremely difficult to give up. In the United States, four out of five smokers say they want to "kick the habit"; each year fewer than one in ten succeed. To see why, it is necessary to understand the effects of tobacco's most powerful ingredient: nicotine.

Nicotine is an alkaloid poison found in tobacco leaves that defends the plant against insect attack. Nicotine affects the nervous systems of insects and is sometimes an ingredient of insecticides. When small doses of pure nicotine are given to rats, the result is instant death.

A cigarette contains an average of eight to nine milligrams of nicotine. However, some of this stays in the unsmoked remainder—the "butt" of the cigarette—and some of it escapes into the air with the smoke. While the amount of nicotine inhaled with each puff is not poisonous, it does have powerful effects on a smoker's nervous system. In fact, nicotine often causes a first-time smoker to feel dizzy and nauseous.

When tobacco smoke is held in the mouth, and not inhaled into the lungs, some nicotine is absorbed through the mucous membranes of the mouth and enters the bloodstream. The blood carrying the nicotine flows to the heart and is then pumped to the brain. Nicotine from chewing tobacco and snuff follows a similar route. However, when nicotine is drawn into the lungs, it passes more quickly into the bloodstream and on to the brain. Often less than ten seconds after a smoker inhales tobacco smoke, a tiny dose of nicotine arrives at his or her brain.

Once in the brain, molecules of nicotine stimulate the release of chemicals called neurotransmitters—substances that speed communication between nerve cells. For example, the release of a neurotransmitter called dopamine produces feelings of pleasure and suppresses appetite. Release of one called beta-endorphin reduces anxiety.

Nicotine is a mood-altering drug with complex effects. Unlike such mood-altering substances as alcohol and cocaine, it does not impair a user's performance—in fact, it tends to increase alertness slightly and may cause a small improvement on memory and attention tests. Yet sometimes nicotine acts as a sedative, bringing feelings of relaxation. In his book *Cigarettes Are Sublime,* Richard Klein wrote, "At different moments, under differing conditions, a cigarette may be smoked for its capacity to steel one's concentration, to focus on a fact in the world; at other times its power to provide release and relaxation, to encourage daydreaming, may be its principal value."

Smokers learn to regulate their doses of nicotine. When they take a shallow puff of smoke, this increases their feelings of alertness. When they suck smoke deep into their lungs, this tends to relax them.

While nicotine can give a person a feeling of pleasure, of well-being, the pleasure is fleeting. In fact, many smokers say that only the first cigarette of the day gives them the full rush of pleasure that nicotine can provide. Just about the time a smoker finishes a cigarette, the nicotine level in the blood peaks, then begins to decline. The drug is gradually removed from the bloodstream in the liver and is eventually excreted with urine.

As the level of nicotine in the blood drops, the smoker begins to experience unpleasant symptoms, beginning with feeling irritated and craving nicotine. Unless the person aims to give up tobacco, the craving is easily satisfied with a dose of nicotine from another cigarette. A pack of twenty cigarettes provides about two hundred little jolts or "hits" of nicotine. In a year's time, a pack-a-day smoker takes seventy thousand hits of nicotine. All of these little "rewards" powerfully reinforce a person's desire to smoke.

Researchers have found that people who have used tobacco for a few months begin to develop a tolerance for the nicotine drug: Their nerve cells become less responsive to nicotine; their bodies remove the drug from their bloodstream more rapidly. Tolerance to nicotine also builds up daily so that a person may have to smoke more cigarettes late in the day to get the desired effect. However, all experienced smokers become adept—without thinking about it— at maintaining the level of nicotine they need in their blood.

The level of nicotine needed varies from person to person. Some maintain a comfortable nicotine level with about a dozen cigarettes a day; others need four dozen. A person's need for nicotine varies somewhat with his or her personality, activities, and surroundings. A highly anxious person in a stressful job may rely on nicotine to relieve stress. Also, being with other smokers often prompts a person to light a cigarette even if his or her blood carries a comfortable level of nicotine. Rituals, like always having a cigarette before or after a meal, become a key part of smoking behavior.

Survey after survey of smokers find that most of them—eight or even nine out of ten—want to quit. A small percentage of tobacco users find quitting to be fairly easy, but most do not. A typical smoker usually tries and fails several times before succeeding. Every year, one of every three smokers in the United States tries to quit. Ninety percent of these people fail by year's end. Even those who succeed in not smoking for a year are in danger of resuming. A third of them become cigarette smokers again.

Though many smokers do not admit it, often their main moti-

WITHDRAWAL SYMPTOMS

Anxiety
Craving cigarettes
Depression
Difficulty concentrating
Disorientation
Dizziness
Eating more than usual
Fatigue
Headaches

Heart palpitations
Impatience
Insomnia
Irritability
Restlessness
Stomach or bowel problems
Sweating
Tremors

Most smokers want to quit, but they face the challenge of dealing with some of these powerful nicotine withdrawal symptoms. The symptoms diminish with time, but a craving for nicotine may last for years.

vation for continuing is not to feel pleasure but to avoid pain—the unpleasant feelings caused by giving up nicotine. In addition to craving nicotine, a person who tries to give up tobacco may suffer from nervousness, irritability, drowsiness, headaches, intestinal upsets, sleep disturbances, and increased appetite. These symptoms are most intense for about a week. The craving for nicotine may persist for weeks, months, or, for some, several years. Some former smokers still feel cravings for tobacco nine years after quitting.

Smokers sometimes refer to a cigarette as a "fix." They say they're "hooked" on nicotine. These are terms that originated with such drugs as heroin and cocaine. Is a tobacco user a nicotine addict? Is nicotine an addictive drug? These questions have been debated and studied for decades and became a major issue again in the mid-1990s, when the U.S. Food and Drug Administration began to consider whether tobacco should be regulated as an addictive drug. Grown on farms, tobacco has always been considered an agricultural product, like corn or broccoli, rather than a drug.

In 1964, a report on tobacco and smoking by the United States Surgeon General stated that smoking was a habit, not an addiction. However, later that same year the World Health Organization dropped this distinction between a habit-forming drug and an addicting drug. In 1988, a report by U.S. Surgeon General C. Everett Koop warned that nicotine is as addictive as heroin and cocaine. Based on the results of more than two thousand scientific studies, the report reflected the growing belief among experts that the use of tobacco was not simply a habit but was a powerful addiction.

At that time a spokesperson for the Tobacco Institute, which represents the tobacco industry, said that the report "contradicts common sense. Smoking is truly a personal choice that can be stopped if and when a person decides to do so."

Another tobacco industry spokesperson said, "The term *addiction* is a debased coin worth nothing at all. You even see references to viewing sports as being addictive."

True, the term is used loosely in conversation. But experts on health have a more precise definition. Dr. Lynn T. Kozlowski, an addiction expert at Pennsylvania State University, said that addiction can be defined as "the repeated use of a psychoactive drug which is difficult to stop." Addictive drugs are hard to give up for one or more reasons—because they produce a powerful, enticing "high," for example, or because they cause disturbing withdrawal feelings.

The World Health Organization and the American Psychiatric Association agree that nine factors must be considered in determining whether a substance is addictive. Although nicotine does not affect a user's mind as dramatically as does cocaine or heroin, it ranks high in other factors. For example, smokers become dependent on nicotine, they develop a tolerance for it, and they suffer withdrawal symptoms when they try to quit or when circumstances force them to be without nicotine for a while. These are key factors in identifying addiction.

A number of studies have been done that prove nicotine is the addicting substance in tobacco. In one conducted in the early 1980s, nicotine was injected into volunteers' veins rather than having them inhale it with tobacco smoke. Individuals reported they felt the same effects as they usually did from smoking. They were able to tell when they were injected with a placebo instead of nicotine. And they also could tell researchers when they had received a low dose or a higher dose of the drug.

In another investigation, volunteers were able to give themselves nicotine injections whenever they wanted. They were denied the usual factors that are part of smoking: the taste of tobacco, the feel of a cigarette in their mouths, the presence (or pressure) of fellow smokers. Nevertheless, their pattern of taking nicotine by injection was similar to their normal smoking behavior. The other factors

Social situations sometimes prompt people to smoke more than they would if alone.

associated with smoking were important to the smokers, but their absence did not keep the volunteers from maintaining their nicotine addiction.

In 1994, Dr. Edythe London of the National Institute of Drug Abuse summarized the research that had been done proving nicotine to be an addictive substance. "Since the 1980s we've shown that when you give the nicotine, it gets to the brain, interacts with specific receptors in the brain, and has distinct effects on the brain. All cigarettes are, are a sophisticated system for delivering the drug."

Nicotine increases heart rate and blood pressure, and these

effects might increase the likelihood of heart attacks in people with weakened hearts. It may also do psychological damage—making the smoker feel powerless to be free of it, and so lowering the person's self-esteem. Yet compared with alcohol, heroin, cocaine, and other addictive substances, nicotine by itself seems to be a fairly harmless drug.

However, there is no doubt that other substances in tobacco do great harm, each year causing more than four hundred thousand deaths in the United States alone. These toxic chemicals are described in the next chapter.

After planting, tobacco is often fertilized and sprayed with insecticides, adding to the hundreds of chemicals that are present in tobacco leaves.

3 DEATH IN SMALL DOSES

"In every puff there is a little taste of death. . . ."
—Richard Klein, *Cigarettes Are Sublime*

Leaves of tobacco, like those of many other plants, naturally contain hundreds of chemical compounds. The process of farming usually adds traces of fertilizers and pesticides to the leaves. Then the process of manufacturing cigarettes or other tobacco products adds more chemicals, such as flavorings. Finally, the process of burning tobacco changes the chemistry of all these ingredients. When a smoker inhales, drawing oxygen into the burning tip of a cigarette, the burning area becomes a miniature furnace, reaching almost two thousand degrees Fahrenheit and producing new compounds. Some are deadly.

One of the most dangerous is tar. When organic materials, such as bits of tobacco leaves, are burned, the end product contains little particles, some of them microscopic. This is tar. Some brands of cigarettes are advertised as "low tar." When burned, their ingredients produce less tar than other cigarettes. However, such cigarettes have less tobacco flavor than normal, so smokers tend to inhale the smoke from such cigarettes very deeply. This defeats the purpose of reducing tar.

When smoke from burning tobacco is inhaled, particles of tar fill the air sacs, called alveoli, of the lungs. This can lead to such chronic lung diseases as bronchitis and emphysema. Cigarette smokers are five times as likely as nonsmokers to die from these diseases. Tar also causes lung cancer.

Another deadly ingredient of tobacco smoke is carbon monoxide gas. Like tar, it results from burning, especially burning in a place where the oxygen supply is limited. Oxygen is restricted inside a cigarette, and this gives rise to carbon monoxide gas. Smokers inhale this gas into their lungs. As it passes through the alveoli into the bloodstream, carbon monoxide combines with hemoglobin, the substance in blood that usually carries oxygen to all parts of the body, including the brain.

The bond between carbon monoxide and hemoglobin is strong. As a smoker continues to inhale more and more of this gas, less free hemoglobin is available to carry oxygen. This can trigger an irregular heartbeat and, over time, damage the heart. In the brain, carbon monoxide can adversely affect vision, timing, coordination, and decision making.

Tobacco smoke also contains radioactive substances. They include lead-210 and polonium-210, the latter reaching tobacco plants from phosphate fertilizers. According to the National Council of Radiation Protection, a person smoking a pack and a half (thirty cigarettes) a day is exposed to more radiation from polonium-210 than is permitted by safety rules for workers in nuclear power plants. Tobacco grown in areas of radon-rich rocks and soils may also contain radioactive radon. Like particles of tar, radioactive substances are known to cause cancers.

Tobacco smoke also contains sixty known or suspected carcinogens—substances or other factors that cause cancer. One is a gas called benzopyrene. People smoking two packs of cigarettes a day inhale nearly twenty times the amount of benzopyrene that they would receive by breathing the polluted air of a city such as Los Angeles.

Smoking tobacco is an act of self-pollution. Some of the effects of smoking begin to appear soon after people become addicted to nicotine. These individuals begin to have more colds and other respiratory diseases. Their lungs are less efficient at delivering oxygen to blood that flows to their brains, organs, and muscles. In athletics and other activities where healthy lung capacity is vital, smokers are handicapped.

The greatest damage caused by tobacco use usually develops slowly. People may smoke for three decades before symptoms of cancers and serious heart disease appear. This can give smokers— especially young people—a false sense of security. Here is a dose of reality: Smokers live several years less than nonsmokers, and each cigarette a person smokes subtracts several minutes from his or her life.

Like cancers and the other deadly diseases tobacco causes, the evidence of tobacco's harm developed slowly. In 1919, a surgeon in a St. Louis hospital asked his medical students to observe the au-

On the basketball court a smoker is a handicapped player.

topsy on a dead patient. The man had died of lung cancer, a disease so rare that the doctor felt that his students might not see it again. Alas, within a few decades, a thoracic (chest) surgeon could see hundreds of patients with lung cancer each year. In the first half of the twentieth century, doctors began to notice that nonsmokers had better health than smokers, but scientific research on the effects of smoking did not begin in earnest until the 1950s.

Smoking, especially smoking cigarettes, grew tremendously in the first half of the twentieth century. Several factors contributed to the steady growth of tobacco use, but a key one was advertising. For the first time, cigarette manufacturers began to advertise nationwide, and there were no legal constraints on the "benefits" they could claim for their products. Cigarette advertisements claimed that smoking was glamorous and sophisticated—an image today's ads continue to project. The ads featured popular athletes and movie stars. Some advertisements quoted doctors and claimed that cigarettes helped smokers control weight, digest food, and fend off colds. And during times of war, some advertisements connected smoking with patriotism.

During World War I (1914–1918), cigarettes were given to every U.S. soldier and sailor as part of his daily rations. This policy was continued during World War II (1939–1945) and during other military actions of the United States until the 1970s. Some military leaders called cigarettes "every soldier's best friend"; because of nicotine's mind-altering effects, it combated both boredom and stress. Thus, with the government's encouragement, many thousands of young men became addicted to nicotine.

In the first half of the twentieth century, movie and sports stars, and even medical doctors, endorsed cigarette smoking.

So did many young women who were part of the war effort. Early in the twentieth century, women smoked in private if at all because smoking was considered unladylike. Then, in the 1920s, after World War I ended, advertisements began to be aimed at women, and cigarette brands were designed to appeal to them. More women took up smoking, though society still frowned on it. Until the early 1950s, motion pictures made in the United States did not show women smoking.

In the 1942 film classic *Casablanca,* for example, the male actors always seem to have a cigarette in their mouths. The women do not smoke. (The male lead of this film, Humphrey Bogart, smoked heavily in real life too; he died of lung cancer at the age of fifty-seven.) However, films made in Hollywood did not reflect reality. By midcentury, women in the United States were smoking as freely as men. They too began to suffer the consequences.

Even while some medical doctors were allowing themselves to be quoted in tobacco advertisements, others began to link tobacco use with deadly disease. Doctors in the United States, England, and Europe reported increased cases of lung cancer. By 1950, studies of the life-styles of lung cancer victims revealed that most had been longtime smokers. In 1953, the *New England Journal of Medicine* announced that the evidence linking smoking and lung cancer was "so strong as to be considered proof within the everyday meaning of the word."

Nevertheless, cigarette consumption in the United States continued to rise; in 1966, 42 percent of adults and a majority of men smoked. That year, however, marked a turning point. President John F. Kennedy had ordered the U.S. Surgeon General's office to review all scientific studies of tobacco use and health. Surgeon General Luther Terry's report, *Smoking and Health,* issued in January 1964, declared that smoking contributed heavily to hundreds of thousands of deaths each year from heart disease, lung disease, and cancer, particularly among men. At that time, relatively few women had smoked long enough to suffer such harm; now women die in great numbers from the same diseases.

The public perception of smoking and tobacco use began to change. Many more smokers tried to quit. Many failed at first but eventually succeeded. Meanwhile, increasing numbers of young people decided not to begin smoking. The percentage of smokers in the U.S. population began to drop. By the mid-1990s, it had fallen to about 25 percent of people over eighteen.

In the 1970s, the American Cancer Society and the American Heart Association started sponsoring antismoking advertisements. Schools began teaching students about the risks of tobacco use. And the U.S. government considered laws aimed to discourage smoking. However, vigorous lobbying by the tobacco industry and efforts by senators and representatives from tobacco-growing states were successful in blocking the toughest legislation. When it became clear that a law calling for a health warning on cigarette packages would be passed, they were able to weaken the message. Beginning in 1965, these words were printed on the sides of cigarette packs: "Caution: Cigarette smoking may be hazardous to your health."

As evidence of tobacco's harm continued to grow, tougher laws were passed. The health warnings on cigarette packages were made stronger and more specific. Beginning in 1971, the same warnings had to be printed on cigarette advertisements in magazines and newspapers and on billboards. That same year, cigarette advertising was also banned from radio and television. Although the tobacco industry lobbied against this ban, tobacco promoters were actually pleased with the end result: Effective radio and television antismoking advertisements also ceased. The public service ads had been allowed by the Federal Communication Commission to counter tobacco ads, and they ended when there were no more tobacco ads to counter.

Since the 1950s, when medical researchers first began to claim that smoking was killing people, the tobacco industry's basic defense has been to deny the claim and to attack the evidence. Scientists supported by the tobacco industry and spokespeople for the Tobacco Institute said the epidemic of lung cancer in the United States could be the result of "air pollution, viruses, food additives, occupational hazards, and stress." Furthermore, they said, people who smoke might have some characteristics that made them likely to develop cancer. Tobacco was not to blame.

The tobacco industry's main criticism of the research on its product's dangers is that there is no direct proof of cause and effect. For example, if someone dies of a gunshot wound, investigators can usually say with great certainty, "This bullet was the cause of death." However, when a smoker dies of lung cancer, other cancers, or heart disease, investigators cannot point to a specific cigarette or even to decades of smoking as the cause with the same degree of certainty.

Through the years, representatives of the tobacco industry have made statements like these: "The same thing that is wrong with the first study is wrong with the thirty thousandth. It just shows an association, not causation." And: "There is no conclusive laboratory or clinical evidence that cigarettes cause any human diseases with which they have been statistically related. So we are left with statistical associations.... The primary basis for the medical case against tobacco is a hypothesis based on statistics."

Actually, the case against smoking is much more than statistics. It includes the visible damage to lungs and hearts that is revealed during autopsies of smokers. It also includes research on laboratory animals. Results from studies using rats, mice, and other mammals have proved to be good predictors of certain diseases in humans.

In many studies, different compounds from tobacco tar were spread on the skin of laboratory rats to see whether tumors formed. This helped scientists learn which substances in tobacco were carcinogenic. Since the cells of mice and humans are quite similar,

Machines that "smoke" cigarettes have been used to measure the amount of tar inhaled by real smokers.

scientists believe that the tobacco substances that cause cancer in mice also cause cancer in people.

Some researchers forced such mammals as dogs and rabbits to "smoke" cigarettes. Very few of the test animals developed lung cancer—a result that pleased the tobacco industry. However, researchers observed that the animals learned quickly to take shallow breaths, barely inhaling the smoke. Instead of lung cancer, they developed tumors of the larynx (voice box) in their throats. Commenting on these observations, a lung cancer expert said, "There is no animal stupid enough to smoke except man. When we find an animal that will inhale cigarette smoke as deeply as man, all the evidence indicates they will get the same tumors as man."

When the tobacco industry attacks "statistical associations" between smoking and death, it attacks the main evidence against smoking. Deaths and their causes, hospital treatments, and other health-related statistics are recorded by county health departments and other government agencies. These records are the basis of epidemiological studies, which explore the relations between disease-causing agents and populations.

The term *epidemiology* means the study of epidemics, which are widespread diseases. The very first epidemiological study, conducted in London in the mid-nineteenth century, is a good example of this research. At that time, many people were dying of cholera, and a doctor named John Snow suspected that the disease was caused by something in the water supply. He learned that people in one area of London were served by two main water sources: either a heavily

Dogs have been forced to smoke in order to study the health effects of tobacco. In an advertisement from the Minnesota Department of Health, this collie was posed to show how silly smoking looks.

polluted stretch of the Thames River or a much cleaner, upstream area of the river. When cholera struck in 1854, Snow visited the homes of victims to learn where their water came from. There were nearly nine times as many cholera deaths in homes where people drank the polluted water.

The results of epidemiological studies are not always so clear-cut. The causes of uncommon diseases may be hard to pin down; sometimes the results of an epidemiological study of one population, or group, are contradicted by the results from another population. For example, a U.S. study found no link between electromagnetic fields from power lines and the incidence of leukemia among utility workers. Yet the results of a similar study in Canada and France *did* seem to reveal such a link.

The results of some epidemiological studies are not very trustworthy because there aren't many disease victims in a population or because it is difficult to learn about their exposure to a disease-causing agent. However, these problems do not affect most epidemiological studies of smoking. Large populations of smokers and of nonsmokers are available. From interviews with smokers themselves, or with the families and co-workers of smokers who have died, it is possible to get fairly accurate information about their past smoking habits. Thousands of epidemiological studies may be "just statistics" to the tobacco industry, but to medical scientists they are powerful evidence of tobacco's harm. The link between smoking and certain diseases is as firmly established as any in medicine.

OPPOSITE: Though smoking does mar a person's looks, this poster from the American Cancer Society emphasizes that the most deadly damage occurs within.

Here is how some of the statistics add up: More than 434,000 people in the United States die each year—about fifty every hour—from smoking-related diseases. Worldwide the annual death toll is at least three million. More than one out of every six deaths in the United States is due to cigarette smoking. These deaths include 30 percent of all cancer deaths (87 percent of lung cancer deaths), 21 percent of deaths from heart disease, and 18 percent of deaths from strokes. Tobacco's annual cost, in terms of health care and time lost from work, is estimated at seventy billion dollars in the United States. The act of smoking has other costs too. According to the National Fire Data Center in Maryland, each year 38 percent of all accidental fires are started from cigarettes.

People who smoke cigars or pipes usually do not inhale smoke deeply. Their rate of premature death is about half that of cigarette smokers. Similarly, people who chew tobacco or hold a wad of snuff inside their cheeks do not inhale, but they cannot escape all the deadly substances in tobacco. They suffer from cancers of the mouth, esophagus, and throat.

The death toll from tobacco use is not spread evenly through a population of people who smoke. Some smokers face a greater risk than others because they smoke more cigarettes each day. Work conditions are also a factor. For example, both cigarettes and asbestos cause lung cancer, so smokers working in the asbestos industry have a very high cancer rate. Other industries where smokers face a greater than normal cancer risk include coal and metal mining, as well as petrochemical, pesticide, and cotton textile manufacturing.

In general, blue-collar workers are exposed to more pollution and disease-causing agents on the job than white-collar workers. Polluting themselves with tobacco smoke just threatens their health even more.

Smoke drifts into the air from an idling cigarette—but not harmlessly. Nearly 90 percent of nonsmokers have some residues of cigarette smoke in their blood.

4 INNOCENT BYSTANDERS

"Children just should not be around people smoking."

—Dr. Ross Brownson
St. Louis University School of Public Health

We have all read the terrible news or seen reports on television: A fire, started by a cigarette, has filled a house or apartment with smoke and flames. A family loses its home and sometimes people die. Sometimes the dead are children. And the survivors may include young children who are scarred for life.

This is indeed a tragedy because, after all, the children are innocent bystanders—nonsmokers who die or suffer for the rest of their lives because of the carelessness of a smoker. But during the 1980s and 1990s, scientists learned of something equally tragic. Many millions of innocent bystanders are being harmed by cigarettes, not because they are victims of fires but simply because they are exposed to cigarette smoke. These people include the spouses, co-workers, and children of smokers, and even fetuses in the wombs of women who smoke.

Almost everyone inhales some air that contains cigarette smoke. This is called passive or involuntary smoking. Scientists call the smoke itself environmental tobacco smoke (ETS). In the second half of the twentieth century, as medical researchers learned of the terrible harm smokers do to themselves, they observed that the health of nonsmokers, including children, seemed to suffer from smoke too. Doctors noticed, for example, that children whose parents smoked seemed to have more colds, bronchitis, and other respiratory infections than children of nonsmokers. They also observed that babies born of mothers who smoked seemed less healthy than babies of nonsmoking mothers.

Medical researchers began to look into this. They discovered that many babies had been, in a sense, smoking cigarettes before they were born. Soon after a woman becomes pregnant, the developing embryo and later the fetus within her receives nicotine, carbon monoxide, and other chemicals from her cigarettes. Carried by the mother's bloodstream, the chemicals cross the placenta, the organ through which oxygen and nutrients reach the unborn child.

Nicotine causes blood vessels to narrow. Carbon monoxide reduces the amount of oxygen in the blood. Together both chemicals reduce the amount of oxygen that gets to the embryo or fetus. Each cigarette smoked temporarily deprives the embryo or fetus of the oxygen that is vital for normal development, especially of its brain and nervous system. So it is not surprising to learn that children of mothers who smoke have lower intelligence scores than children of nonsmokers. In a 1994 study, preschool children whose mothers smoked ten or more cigarettes a day during pregnancy scored an

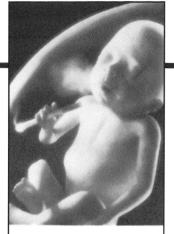

Though a human fetus does not smoke as shown in this poster from the American Cancer Society, it does take in chemicals from a mother who smokes. These chemicals harm its health and threaten its very survival.

average of nine points lower on IQ tests than preschool children of nonsmoking mothers. Also, research at Emory University in Atlanta revealed in 1996 that pregnant women who smoked at least a pack of cigarettes a day were 85 percent more likely than nonsmoking women to give birth to a mentally retarded child.

Some embryos or fetuses of smoking women never become live babies, because women who smoke regularly have a higher incidence of stillbirths and miscarriages than nonsmokers. They also tend to have more premature births. At birth, even those infants who are not premature weigh about seven ounces below normal. Birth weight is a key factor in the survival of an infant. Starting life with below-normal weight, a baby born to a smoker is more likely to die in infancy than one born to a nonsmoker.

One tragedy that every parent fears is crib death, or Sudden Infant Death Syndrome (SIDS), in which an apparently healthy baby dies in its sleep. While the cause or causes of SIDS are still not completely understood, smoking is known to be a factor. Babies born to smoking mothers are three times more likely to die of SIDS than the babies of nonsmokers.

A baby continues to "smoke" if it is nursed by a mother who smokes, because it receives chemicals from cigarettes in its mother's milk. Even if a baby delivered by a smoker is raised in a nonsmoking home, the harm done before birth may affect the child's mental abilities and overall health. In most cases, of course, a child born to a smoking mother is raised in a home where one or both parents smoke and the whole family inhales environmental tobacco smoke.

This ETS has two sources. One is the "used," or secondhand, smoke that people exhale after they inhale mainstream smoke (smoke from their burning cigarettes). The other source of ETS is called sidestream smoke. It rises from the burning tip of a cigarette when a smoker inhales or when the cigarette burns slowly in an ashtray or smoker's hand. Most tobacco smoke in a home or other enclosed space enters the air this way.

Tobacco that burns slowly is burned less completely than mainstream smoke and differs from it chemically. The amount of nicotine in mainstream and sidestream smoke is about the same. However, sidestream smoke is dirtier and more dangerous than mainstream smoke. It contains much higher amounts of benzene, polonium-210, cadmium, and other chemicals known to cause cancer. (The table on the opposite page shows more details about the chemistry of mainstream and sidestream smoke.)

SIDESTREAM SMOKE

Substance	Increase in substance in sidestream smoke compared with mainstream smoke
Polonium-210	1 to 4 times
Benzo(a)pyrene	2.5 to 3.5 times
Hydrazine	3 times
1,3-butadiene	3 to 6 times
Benzene	5 to 10 times
N-nitrosopyrrolidine	6 to 30 times
Cadmium	7.2 times
Nickel	13 to 30 times
N-nitrosodimenthylamine	20 to 100 times
Aniline	30 times
2-Naphthylamine	30 times
4-Aminobiphenyl	31 times
N-nitrodiethylamine	up to 40 times

Sidestream cigarette smoke differs from the mainstream smoke that is inhaled. It contains higher concentrations of several known or suspected cancer-causing substances.

Source: U.S. Occupational Safety and Health Administration

The poisons of sidestream smoke do become greatly diluted in the air as smoke wafts away from a cigarette. However, the concentration of these chemicals increases in the air of homes, workplaces, restaurants, bars, and other places where ventilation is poor. In such environments sidestream smoke can become a real threat to nonsmokers. The more of this smoke inhaled, the greater the risk.

Some homes and other environments are much worse than others. Many people who wait on tables in restaurants and serve drinks in bars work long hours in an often-smoky environment. Their risk of getting lung cancer is 50 percent higher than that of other people.

Dr. Katharine Hammond, an environmental health expert at the University of California at Berkeley, made a careful study of certain ingredients of sidestream smoke that a nonsmoker would inhale while working in an office with smoking colleagues. During one month, she concluded, "The nonsmoker is getting as much benzene as a smoker gets in smoking six cigarettes; as much 4ABP, a known human carcinogen, as if smoking seventeen cigarettes; and as much NDMA, the potent animal carcinogen, as one who smoked seventy-five cigarettes."

Children growing up in homes polluted by cigarette smoke suffer from more nose, throat, and ear infections, pneumonia, bronchitis, and asthma attacks than normal. In 1986, a report on ETS by the National Research Council concluded that passive smoke inhaled during childhood might permanently stunt growth and lung development and possibly increase the risk of lung disease when the children become adults. The report urged that infants and children be protected from exposure to tobacco smoke. Other researchers have stated the case against secondary smoke even more dramatically. Dr. William Cahan of the Memorial Sloan-Kettering Cancer Center in New York City called the exposure of fetuses and children to cigarette smoking a form of child abuse.

Smoking by one parent has become an issue in divorce courts when children are involved. In most cases, a nonsmoking parent has been successful in insisting that the other parent give the children a smoke-free environment. In some cases that involved children with asthma, custody was given to the nonsmoking parent.

Children and adults who live with a smoker may consider themselves nonsmokers, but they actually inhale a considerable amount of tobacco smoke each day.

This happened in the case of an eight-year-old girl in Sacramento, California. Thanks to her mother's smoking, *she* was "smoking" eight cigarettes a day from the air in their home.

For nonsmokers in general, young and old, tobacco smoke may irritate eyes and throats and cause headaches. Starting in the early 1980s, evidence began to emerge that indicated smoke causes much more serious damage, and death. Epidemiological researchers focused on nonsmoking women who developed lung cancer and investigated whether they were wives of men who smoked. Researchers also looked at the health of husbands of woman smokers and of people exposed to smoke at work.

The early studies reported conflicting results: Some found that passive smoking increased the risk of lung cancer, while others did not. However, by 1986 U.S. Surgeon General C. Everett Koop found the evidence strong enough to warn that simply breathing ETS could cause lung cancer.

This report was challenged by the tobacco industry, which had recognized in the late 1970s that people were becoming concerned about passive smoking. This alarmed the tobacco companies, not about possible danger to people, but about danger to their business. If people believed that cigarette smoke in the air threatened their health, this could lead to restrictions on smoking indoors, to more people quitting smoking, to fewer people starting.

In advertisements and statements to the news media, the tobacco industry attacked the scientific evidence. Scientists supported by the Tobacco Institute pointed out flaws and inconsistencies. Advertisements then claimed that there was disagreement among scientists; therefore there was no need for any restrictions on indoor smoking. For a time, there *was* debate among reputable scientists about the strength of the earliest studies of passive smoking. However, results from more epidemiological research erased doubt.

In 1992, the Environmental Protection Agency (EPA) reported that passive smoking causes as many as 3,300 lung cancer deaths each year. This is a small number, compared with the smokers who die of cancer. The spouses of smokers may face a one-in-five-hundred chance of developing lung cancer, while smokers face between a one-in-ten and a one-in-twenty chance. Still, cigarette smoke in the air can be as dangerous as benzene and other known carcinogens that are already regulated by air pollution laws.

The EPA's findings were based on thirty epidemiological studies from around the world. Since then other research has strengthened the case against tobacco smoke in the air we breathe. As of 1995, twenty-six of thirty-three studies showed a link between ETS and lung cancer. Research also showed that nonsmokers exposed to their spouses' smoke have an increased chance of dying of heart disease. Overall, passive smoking causes an estimated 47,000 people to die of heart attacks and 150,000 others to suffer nonfatal heart attacks in the United States each year.

Even when faced with these findings, the tobacco industry continued to claim that scientists disagreed about whether passive smoking was harmful. But as Dr. Stanton Glantz, a tobacco researcher at the University of California in San Francisco, said in 1995, "If we didn't have the tobacco companies spending millions of dollars to confuse the facts, this issue would be an open-and-shut

In full-page magazine and newspaper advertisements, the tobacco industry criticized the scientific evidence that led to health warnings about passive smoking.

case. The fact is that passive smoking causes lung cancer."

Over the years, the tobacco industry has indeed spent many millions, not just in nationwide advertisements but in cities, counties, and states that were taking steps to protect people from ETS. While tobacco industry lobbyists often succeeded in slowing the pace of regulation, or in stalling or weakening proposed ordinances, they did not stop them. By the mid-1990s, nearly all states restricted smoking in restaurants and in workplaces. Many private companies now forbid smoking indoors. This not only pleases nonsmokers but has a practical, economic side: It reduces the cost of medical insurance and sick leave due to smoking-related illnesses and diseases. Thousands of cities and towns have their own laws that limit or ban smoking in public buildings, public transit, hospitals, museums, shopping malls, restaurants, workplaces—even jails and prisons. And since 1988, the Federal Aviation Administration has prohibited smoking on passenger airlines in the United States.

The tobacco industry continued to claim that there was no trustworthy scientific evidence that passive smoking was harmful. However, in the late 1970s it began to try another tactic: diverting attention from passive smoking by promoting the cause of "smokers' rights." Advertisements now focused on the issue of individual rights against excessive government regulation.

A 1994 advertisement, paid for by the R. J. Reynolds Tobacco Company, warned of proposed cigarette tax increases and tougher

Smoking is now restricted or banned in many workplaces, and in other areas where people gather.

regulations on smoking. "The Government," claimed the ad, "is attempting to prohibit smoking in America.... If they are successful in their bid to abolish cigarettes will they then pursue other targets? Will alcohol be next?... Will books, movies and music get the treatment? Who knows where it will end?"

Advertisements by Philip Morris, the chief competitor of R. J. Reynolds, stated that "most Americans prefer accommodation and common courtesy to more regulations and outright bans."

The tobacco industry helped set up "grassroots" groups of diehard smokers, such as the Smoker's Rights Alliance of Mesa, Arizona. As this group saw it, smoking is a civil rights issue, and people in the United States should be free to enjoy this habit. Nonsmokers who wanted smoking restricted were pictured as rude radicals, trampling on the rights of smokers. Why couldn't they be more understanding of smokers?

"Well, forgive me for being rude," wrote columnist Ellen Goodman, "but 'understanding' the smoker sharing your air rights is a

The tobacco industry provides funds and materials, such as bumper stickers, to local groups, including owners of bars and restaurants who oppose regulations on smoking by their customers.

bit like giving someone permission to step on your feet, or burn poison-ivy incense. It's important to keep the characters straight. The smoker is the aggressor. The nonsmoker is the defender."

A January 1993 editorial in the *New York Times* agreed that smoking did involve rights: "Smoking does, therefore, involve rights, and it is the smokers who are the violators…. No one would grant his neighbor the right to blow tiny amounts of asbestos into a room or sprinkle traces of pesticide onto food. By the same logic, smokers have no right to spew even more noxious clouds into the air around them."

There can be no right to harm other people. Besides, smoking is not really a civil rights issue; it is a health issue. The concept of smokers' rights was raised by the tobacco industry only after it recognized that it was losing the battle for public opinion over the dangers of passive smoking.

Tobacco is an important agricultural crop in several southern states, and is raised in twenty-three states in all.

5 PROMOTING A PRODUCT THAT KILLS

"One of the many bizarre things about the tobacco industry is that its product keeps killing off its customers. With more than 400,000 Americans succumbing every year to the effects of tobacco, industry executives are locked into a perpetual search for new (young) smokers. Their need is as gruesome as it is basic— live ones to replace the dead ones."

—Bob Herbert, columnist, *New York Times*

Tobacco is big business—a $47 billion business in the United States, with a fast-growing foreign market as well. Since the cost of actually manufacturing cigarettes is small, tobacco companies are among the most profitable businesses in the world. Tobacco farming itself is also very profitable. Thanks in part to a U.S. government program that guarantees growers a certain price, tobacco farmers earn $3,500 or more an acre. In contrast, cotton farmers earn about $380 an acre and wheat farmers $100 an acre.

In the United States most tobacco is grown in the South, though twenty-three states and Puerto Rico have tobacco farms. The United States produces seven million tons of tobacco each year; only China grows more. In all, the whole U.S. tobacco industry—growing, processing, manufacturing, distributing, and promoting—provides jobs for about seven hundred thousand people. Not included in this total are other people who benefit from the tobacco industry: scientists who study the health effects of tobacco products, doctors and other health care professionals who treat people harmed by tobacco use, and workers employed by companies that sell products and services that help smokers try to quit. To this list you might also add morticians and others who work in the funeral industry, because, though everyone dies sooner or later, smokers die sooner—on average, eight years sooner.

There are six tobacco-selling companies in the United States; most of them also sell other products that are unrelated to tobacco. About three-quarters of the tobacco market is controlled by two companies, Philip Morris and RJR Nabisco (formerly R. J. Reynolds). Besides tobacco products, RJR Nabisco also sells cookies, cereals, and other foods. Philip Morris owns Kraft General Foods and Miller Beer. Philip Morris, the industry leader, pays income taxes of more than $4 billion a year. Each year it sells at least $4 billion worth of cigarettes overseas. These exports contribute to the U.S. balance of payments (value of exports compared to imports) with foreign nations.

The tobacco industry is a powerful economic force, both nationally and locally, in the six main tobacco-growing states (Virginia,

North Carolina, South Carolina, Georgia, Kentucky, and Florida). Tobacco accounts for more than 20 percent of all agricultural income in some southern states. Indirectly, the tobacco growing and manufacturing process supports farm machinery and fertilizer businesses, as well as gasoline stations, food stores, and many other aspects of the economy.

A declining tobacco business would be a hard blow to the economy of the tobacco-growing states. Therefore, their governors, state legislators, and representatives and senators elected to the U.S. Congress are usually ardent supporters of the tobacco industry. For example, consider a 1989 incident in Kentucky, the nation's leading tobacco grower—and also its leader in the rate of smoking-related deaths. Kentucky legislators threatened to cut the budget of the University of Louisville if it did not loosen some new restrictions on smokers. The university complied, weakening its efforts to protect nonsmoking students and employees.

Sometimes, however, political efforts to help tobacco growers do not please cigarette manufacturers. In the early 1990s, cigarette makers were using increasing amounts of cheaper imported tobacco. American growers protested to their senators and representatives in Washington, D.C., who pushed through a law that required manufacturers to use at least 75 percent homegrown tobacco.

The tobacco industry was once the most effective lobbying force in Washington. Negative public opinion about smoking has changed that. Nevertheless, the industry still wields considerable power and can still block or weaken proposals it opposes. In 1990, a Senate aide said, "The tobacco industry has always been sophisticated, and now it is becoming more sophisticated. They hire the best people money can buy, former congressional or agency staffers, prominent lawyers, people who understand how Congress works."

Each year the tobacco industry contributes about $2.5 million to the political campaigns of members of Congress. While the greatest amounts go to representatives from tobacco states, large sums are also paid to certain congressmen from such states as New York and Michigan. One example is Representative Charles Rangel of Harlem, a largely black district in New York City. Between 1985 and 1995 Rangel received about $50,000 from the tobacco industry, nearly as much as several members of Congress from Georgia, Tennessee, and other tobacco-growing states. Though he votes against the tobacco industry on some issues, he is strongly opposed to increased taxes on cigarettes. He believes that such taxes hurt poor people more than others.

Some antismoking groups say that black lawmakers in particular, including Rangel, should refuse money from tobacco companies, since the death rate from lung disease is 22 percent higher for blacks than whites. However, the tobacco industry spins a tangled web, contributing large sums of money to many black organizations, both nationally and in local districts, including Rangel's—for example, to the Dance Theater of Harlem. According to Dr. Norma Goodwin of Brooklyn, New York, who founded a group that seeks ways for communities to wean themselves from tobacco money, "By supporting the lifeblood of communities, the tobacco companies have almost silenced or paralyzed the leadership who would speak out."

Each year the tobacco industry gives several million dollars to scores of worthy social and arts groups: the United Negro College Fund, the Legal Aid Society, hunger-relief organizations, hospitals, ballet companies, museums… The list goes on and on. This is one of many ways in which the industry tries to create goodwill among the public, community leaders, and politicians—without advertising.

In fact, now the tobacco industry is spending less on direct advertising and more on other ways of marketing. After broadcast

Tobacco's terrible death toll among black people has caused some black leaders to protest cigarette advertisements aimed at blacks.

advertisements were banned in January 1971, cigarette companies relied mostly on ads in magazines and newspapers and on billboards. The millions of dollars that were spent each year on magazine advertisements did more than just promote tobacco use. They caused certain magazines to be less critical of smoking. Research published in 1989 in the *New England Journal of Medicine* concluded that "coverage of smoking and health issues decreased by 65 percent in magazines that carried cigarette advertisements, as compared with a decrease of 29 percent in magazines that did not."

By the mid-1990s, tobacco companies were spending about $700 million annually on advertisements and nearly $4 billion on other forms of marketing. These included cents-off coupons, multiple packs (buy one, get one free), and mail-in merchandising offers, in which consumers get key chains, lighters, watches, T-shirts, caps, sports equipment, and other items by clipping symbols and bar codes from cigarette packaging. Studies have shown these marketing ploys have special appeal to young people. According to a 1992 Gallup poll, half of all teenage smokers and a quarter of teenage nonsmokers owned at least one promotional item from a cigarette company.

Like other producers of consumer products, tobacco companies pay stores to give them shelf space in favorable locations and for displaying signs promoting certain brands. They reach many millions of potential customers in their homes by mail, delivering discount coupons and advertisements. In 1993, Philip Morris had twenty-six million people on its mailing lists.

There are other, more subtle ways of reaching potential smok-

Clothing, sports equipment, and other products that can be purchased only by buying plenty of cigarettes have proved to be popular with young people.

ers, so that people do not realize they are the target of an advertisement. During the 1980s, for example, the Brown and Williamson Tobacco Corporation paid $1 million to movie producers in return for having cigarette packs and billboard advertisements appear in films. In some movies this "product placement" agreement called for actors to smoke. According to the Tobacco Institute, since 1990 tobacco companies no longer make such arrangements, though cigarette brands and advertisements continue to appear prominently in some movies.

Another practice had become common since television advertisements were banned in 1971: putting up cigarette ads in sports stadiums and arenas. In 1990, for instance, cigarette companies had large advertisements in all but two of the major-league baseball stadiums in the United States. Here, and in stadiums and arenas where professional football, basketball, and hockey are played, the ads were usually placed where television viewers were certain to see them. In fact, tobacco companies sometimes paid large fees to ensure that their signs would be on television screens for several minutes during a game.

In 1995 the U.S. Justice Department threatened to sue Philip Morris for willfully violating the law. Assistant Attorney General Frank Hunger said that the ads were an effort to reach young people, by associating sports with smoking. "These professional sports appeal to young people," he said, "and this image advertising can influence young fans' willingness to begin smoking."

A spokesperson for Philip Morris said that the signs were intended to reinforce brand loyalty among existing smokers and to

Forbidden to advertise on television, cigarette companies rented huge signs in sports stadiums. When the games were telecast, the cigarette ads appeared on TV. This violation of the law was finally halted in the mid-1990s.

encourage brand switching. Nevertheless, the company agreed to remove signs that could be seen often during telecasts, and the other tobacco firms were expected to follow.

Even though these signs are being removed, tobacco advertisements continue to be displayed prominently at car races and rodeos, and at rock, jazz, or country music concerts that are sponsored by cigarette brands. And it is no coincidence that cigarette companies began to sponsor certain sporting events in 1971—the year they were barred from advertising on television and radio. Winston, an RJR Nabisco brand, sponsors the Winston Cup auto race. Telecasts show cars painted with cigarette brands, in races named for cigarette brands, speeding around tracks decked with cigarette billboards.

Beginning in 1971, Philip Morris sponsored Virginia Slims women's tennis tournaments. This type of connection between cigarettes and sports was attacked in 1991 by Dr. Louis Sullivan, Secretary of Health and Human Services. During an average tennis match, he said, about a hundred Americans "will die of diseases caused by cigarette smoking."

Dr. Sullivan urged sports promoters and players to shun tobacco's "blood money." Some female professional tennis players defended Philip Morris, saying it had done a lot for women's tennis. This was true, but during the two decades when women's tennis gained in fame and prestige, the lung cancer rate among women also soared. Until 1985 the leading cause of death of women was breast cancer. That year lung cancer became the leading cause of death, a consequence of increased smoking by women. This fact helped health advocates persuade the Women's Tennis Council to end Philip Morris's sponsorship in 1994.

An African-American, Dr. Sullivan made the health of minority populations a priority during his term as Secretary of Health and Human Services. In 1990 he criticized RJR Nabisco for preparing to launch a new cigarette brand called Uptown. The packaging, name, and advertising campaign were aimed at blacks. So was the menthol flavoring, which is preferred by many black smokers. Shortly before Uptown was to be test-marketed in Philadelphia, Dr. Sullivan spoke in that city, saying, "At a time when our people desperately need the message of health promotion, Uptown's message is more disease, more suffering, and more death for a group already bearing more than its share of smoking-related illness and mortality."

Criticism of Uptown also came from the American Cancer Society and from many religious and community organizations in Philadelphia. The test-marketing and the brand were canceled. The company's response: "We regret that a small coalition of antismoking zealots apparently believe that black smokers are somehow different from others who choose to smoke and must not be allowed to exercise the same freedom of choice available to all other smokers. This represents...further erosion of the free enterprise system."

Actually, the only thing unusual about the ill-fated Uptown brand was the manufacturer's admission that it was aiming at black smokers. Especially since smoking has begun to decline in the United States, cigarette manufacturers have analyzed the market and tried to develop brands and advertisements that appeal to certain groups, such as blue-collar workers or affluent women, in order to induce them to switch from a rival company's brand. With fewer adults smoking, the cigarette companies concentrate especially on the groups of people who have the most difficulty quitting: blue-collar workers, women, and blacks.

Another key target is the youth of America. With older customers dying and others managing to quit, young people represent the tobacco industry's main hope of maintaining sales in the United States. Teenagers are the primary source of new smokers. After age twenty almost no one starts.

Nearly all states have laws that forbid selling cigarettes to people under eighteen, but enforcement of those laws is often lax or nonexistent. Also, some underage smokers get cigarettes from vending machines. In 1995, one out of every three high school seniors said they had smoked in the past month; about one out of every five smoked daily. Every day, three thousand Americans reach their eighteenth birthday addicted to tobacco.

This alarms public health advocates because today's youth has had plenty of warnings about the harm in smoking. Why do such large numbers continue to start? In 1995, President Bill Clinton offered this explanation: "Teenagers don't just happen to smoke. They're the victims of billions of dollars of marketing and promotional campaigns designed by top psychologists and advertising experts. These campaigns have one inevitable consequence: to start children on a lifetime habit of addiction to tobacco."

Tobacco companies deny ever aiming any advertisements or other promotions at minors. In a naive sense, this is true; teenagers are not actually shown in advertisements, and cigarette ads do not

Antismoking groups urge that cigarette vending machines be outlawed, to help discourage minors from smoking.

SMOKERS START YOUNG

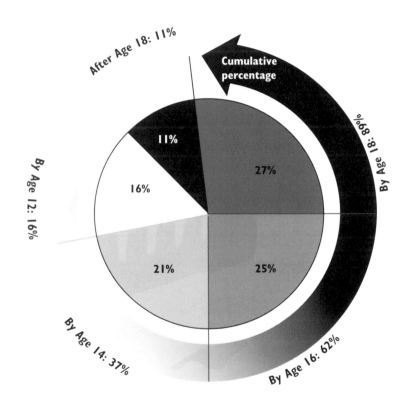

After Age 18: 11%

Cumulative percentage

By Age 18: 89%

11%

27%

16%

By Age 12: 16%

21%

25%

By Age 14: 37%

By Age 16: 62%

This chart shows the results of a 1991 study in which daily smokers were asked when they began smoking. After age eighteen few people begin to smoke.

Source: Office on Smoking and Health, Centers for Disease Control and Prevention

appear in such magazines as *Seventeen.* However, cigarettes are advertised in such magazines as *Sports Illustrated* and *Rolling Stone,* which many teenagers read. Also, young people find the hats and other cigarette promotional items appealing; they attend and watch sports events sponsored by cigarette companies. More basically, teenagers look forward to being independent young adults, and cigarette advertisements that show healthy-looking, attractive young models smoking send the same messages to twelve-year-olds or sixteen-year-olds as they do to twenty-five-year-olds.

An executive who had worked on cigarette advertisements said in 1994: "Successful cigarette advertising involves showing the kind of people most people would like to be, doing the things most people would like to do and smoking up a storm. I don't know any way of doing this that doesn't tempt young people to smoke."

Teenage girls worry a lot about their appearance and weight. In fashion and other women's magazines they see advertisements for cigarettes intended for females. The ads link smoking to fashion, beauty, and slimness; they use such terms as *slim, thin,* and *light.* Like most magazines that feature tobacco advertisements, these magazines rarely print any unpleasant facts about the effects of smoking. Research shows that teenage girls who are extremely weight conscious are more likely than others to start smoking.

Young white females are the fastest-growing group of smokers in the United States. The group that has turned away from tobacco in great numbers is black teenagers. In the mid-1970s both black and white teenagers smoked at about equal rates. By 1993, however, about 23 percent of white teenagers took up regular

Cigarette advertisements emphasize fun and, for young women, slimness, since many teenage girls worry about being what they consider overweight.

smoking while only 4.4 percent of black teenagers did.

The reason for this dramatic change seems to lie in differences between the white and black youth cultures. Among blacks, slimness is less important; black culture permits women to be heavier and still be seen as attractive. Also, according to Dr. Michael Eriksen of the Federal Centers for Disease Control and Prevention in Atlanta, "Blacks seem to be turning off the message from cigarette companies that smoking is cool. For blacks, it no longer provides that function. You hear black teens saying smoking's a white thing."

The notion that smoking is cool has been withering for some time. In 1984, a University of Wisconsin study had students give opinions about photographs of people, some shown with cigarettes, some without. The students rated the people with cigarettes as less sexy, honest, and mature than the same individuals pictured without cigarettes. However, these are the judgments of college students, who, according to studies, are less likely to smoke than teens who are not college-bound.

What type of teens are most likely to become regular smokers? Several studies have revealed that smoking-prone teens usually have low self-esteem and self-image, which makes them vulnerable to peer pressure. Having friends—and especially a best friend—who smoke is often a powerful influence. They tend to be rebellious toward authority. They often suffer from depression. And they are often poor students. One study that compared nonsmoking teenage girls with girls who smoked found that the smokers were more social and less athletic than nonsmokers; they read less and got lower grades.

Having a friend who smokes can lure a nonsmoker into a lifelong addiction to tobacco.

Whether or not they become smokers, young people have some erroneous ideas about smoking in our culture. Smoking was once widely accepted. Now three out of four adults are nonsmokers, and smoking is not socially acceptable in many situations. Nevertheless, studies show that teenagers overestimate the percentage of their peers and adults who smoke. While in reality about a quarter of adolescent students in the cities studied were occasional or regular smokers, students surveyed thought that more than half, even as many as 90 percent, of their peers smoked.

SMOKELESS TOBACCO

Four kinds of smokeless tobacco are made in the United States. Three varieties—loose leaf, plug, and twist—are meant to be chewed. The fourth, oral snuff, made of fine particles of tobacco with added flavoring, is taken by "dipping"—placing a pinch of loose snuff or a little packet of it between the cheek and gums, or beneath the tongue.

Before 1970, old men in rural areas were the main consumers of smokeless tobacco. Since then, however, advertising by U.S. Tobacco, the main manufacturer of snuff, has lured many young males into snuff addiction. By the early 1990s, 11 percent of high school seniors who were surveyed said they had tried smokeless tobacco. Its use is still much more common in rural areas than in cities. In several states, including Alabama, Idaho, Colorado, Montana, and Wyoming, more teenage boys dip snuff than smoke cigarettes.

Many young people believe that smokeless tobacco is safe, or at least much safer than cigarettes. However, the three top-selling brands of snuff (Copenhagen, Skoal fine cut, and Kodiak) contain high levels of nicotine. Regular users become addicted to nicotine, and commonly become cigarette smokers. Snuff also contains several carcinogens. So, besides having yellow teeth and inflamed and receding gums, many snuff dippers soon develop precancerous sores in their mouths. Actual cancers of the mouth or throat appear later; long-term use of smokeless tobacco also leads to ulcers, high blood pressure, and heart disease.

Any person, including a child, entering a convenience store is often confronted with cigarette ads at the door and at the service counter. And minors are often able to buy cigarettes at such stores.

Students who were smokers themselves had the most distorted vision of smoking reality. For example, several thousand Los Angeles–area teenagers who were regular smokers estimated that 55 percent of eighth and ninth graders smoked regularly. In fact, 9 percent and 12 percent of eighth and ninth graders, respectively, were regular smokers when the survey was conducted, in 1988.

Teenagers may believe that smoking is the norm as a result of being bombarded with cigarette advertisements—on billboards, at sporting events and concerts, in magazines that are popular with young adults, and at the entrances and counters of convenience stores and other businesses where adolescents can often buy cigarettes without difficulty. A 1995 study of more than 5,700 such stores in California found that the greatest number of tobacco advertisements were displayed in stores located near schools.

The tobacco industry continues to deny that it is advertising to minors. It urges that existing state laws be strictly enforced, and it gives tobacco retailers signs they can display that warn customers about those laws. The Tobacco Institute offers parents free booklets, including *Tobacco: Helping Youth Say No*. The text of these booklets stresses that children shouldn't smoke; smoking should be an adult decision. The awful damage done by tobacco use is not mentioned, except for a brief reference to "the claims that smoking presents risks to one's health."

In 1995 Philip Morris announced a stepped-up campaign to "keep cigarettes away from kids." Minnesota Attorney General Hubert H. Humphrey III warned that the tobacco industry "had a long history of hypocritical public relations campaigns," and added, "If the tobacco industry is truly interested in keeping cigarettes out of the hands of minors, they should stop spending millions in states like Minnesota to defeat efforts to strengthen laws banning tobacco sales to kids."

In all the disputes about tobacco promotion and its effects on young people, one advertising campaign in particular has drawn heavy criticism. In 1988, RJR Nabisco began promoting Camel cigarettes with a cartoon camel: Joe Camel, a "smooth character." The

Research shows that the Joe Camel cartoon character has been highly successful in luring teenagers to smoke Camel cigarettes.

company said that advertisements, merchandise offers, and so on were aimed at people in their twenties. But Joe Camel's sunglasses, saxophone, and cool clothes appeal to teenagers. In fact, this cartoon animal appeals to children younger than ten years old. A Georgia study found that 91 percent of six-year-olds correctly linked the Joe Camel character with the cigarette it promotes. Other research showed that nearly all teenagers recognized Joe, while only 72 percent of adults did.

In 1994, the Federal Trade Commission denied requests by antismoking groups to prohibit Joe Camel advertisements. Joe continues to appear on billboards, in magazine advertisements, and elsewhere. RJR Nabisco continues to deny that teenagers are the target of Joe Camel. Nevertheless, since Joe Camel first appeared, increasing numbers of underage smokers have chosen Camels as their brand.

Even if they are not the direct target of cigarette promotions, children and teenagers see and remember advertisements and are strongly influenced by them.

A simple decision—to smoke or not—can have a huge effect on the quality and length of a person's life.

6 A SMOKE-FREE SOCIETY?

> "Historians will marvel at the fact that in the last few decades we have been panicking over the alleged health effects of things like DDT..., nitrates in cured meat..., the chemicals in hair dyes. Yet we seem to tolerate a product which kills hundreds of thousands of us every year. No, we just don't tolerate it, we subsidize it and we advertise it and we promote it."
>
> —Dr. Elizabeth Whelan
> American Council on Science and Health

During the last half of the twentieth century, tobacco went from being a substance whose use was widely accepted in everyday life to one whose use was barred in many homes and businesses. It went from being a substance blamed for such minor problems as coughs, bad breath, and stained teeth to one known to cause three million deaths worldwide each year.

In headlines, journalists wondered "How Do Tobacco Executives Live with Themselves?" Scientists who echoed the Tobacco Institute's statements on smoking and disease were viewed with contempt by scientists and health professionals who were knowledgeable about the harm done by tobacco. And the industry was threatened with growing restrictions on the sale and promotion of its products.

Yet, even though its sales in the United States seemed likely to dwindle, the tobacco industry was hopeful. In 1991, Philip Morris assured its stockholders, "Tobacco is a growth industry, and we are gaining in volume and share in markets around the world."

With times tough at home, in the 1980s the tobacco industry began to aim at overseas markets, especially in Asia, and at women in nations where women traditionally did not smoke. In this pursuit of new customers, the industry had a strong helping hand from the U.S. government.

For decades, the U.S. Department of Agriculture has supported the tobacco industry with guaranteed prices for farmers and taxpayer-financed research on tobacco growing. Until 1980 it also sent abroad many millions of dollars' worth of tobacco products under the Food for Peace program. However, in the 1980s, during the administration of President Ronald Reagan, the tobacco industry found a new ally in Washington: the Office of the U.S. Trade Representative. This agency has the power to impose tariffs and other economic punishment on any nation thought to have unfair trade barriers to U.S. products. For many years, Asian countries had trade rules that barred or discouraged cigarette imports. The tobacco industry used its influence in Washington, and the Office of the U.S. Trade Representative demanded that trade barriers be removed. As a result, between 1986 and 1988 huge foreign markets for U.S. cigarettes were opened, and in 1994 Philip Morris gained access to China, which consumes 30 percent of the world's tobacco.

Selling cigarettes abroad is an economic boost in the U.S. balance of payments between exports and imports with other nations. But what about the ethics of a government encouraging export of a poisonous substance whose use it tries to discourage at home? Antismoking groups were dismayed with the government's role in exporting a dangerous, addictive product.

A negotiator for the trade office defended its actions, saying, "It's not as though we are introducing Asia to tobacco. The Chinese manufacture and consume 1.3 trillion cigarettes annually. The market in Taiwan and Korea was established long before any trade negotiations, and they're going to smoke whether the U.S. is exporting cigarettes or not."

In several Asian nations, however, cigarettes were formerly sold through government monopolies that did little or no advertising. Also, people in those countries are not well informed about the link between tobacco use and disease. The U.S. cigarette companies unleashed aggressive advertising campaigns, often using tactics they could not use at home. In Malaysia, cigarette ads have appeared in comic books that are popular with elementary school children. In South Korea, American cigarette brands do not carry the health warnings that are required in the United States. In Taiwan and Japan, the health warning is rather tame: "For the sake of health, don't smoke too much."

Japan permits cigarette advertisements on television, and smoking often is shown in television dramas. Like many nations, Japan

is reluctant to discourage smoking. A government-owned company is the only Japanese company that produces and sells cigarettes. It generates $15 billion in taxes each year, more than any other Japanese company. Smoking was once taboo for Japanese women, but the power of advertisements for women's brands of cigarettes is changing that. Smoking by minors is illegal in Japan, but teenagers can easily buy cigarettes from a half million vending machines. Entering Japan in 1985, American tobacco companies used aggressive sales tactics to capture nearly 20 percent of the Japanese market by 1995.

Throughout Asia, and in developing nations in Africa and South America, young people see billboards and other advertisements that link U.S. cigarettes with an image of the United States—rich, powerful, free. Asked why she smoked Marlboros, a seventeen-year-old girl in Bangkok, Thailand, said that it made her feel "sophisticated and cosmopolitan, like America." Marlboro cigarettes, for her, went with "jeans and denim jackets, Pizza Hut, everything we like about America."

In Thailand, Japan, and other nations, antismoking groups report that earlier progress they had made was washed away by a flood of advertising and other promotions, including free samples, when American cigarette companies arrived. The number of young smokers, especially women, continues to grow. Deaths from lung cancer and heart disease are rising in Asia. In 1992, while physicians warned that a health-care catastrophe loomed ahead in Asia, an executive of RJR Nabisco spoke of that company's expansion abroad, which would "pave the way for a bigger and brighter future."

At home in the 1990s the future of the tobacco industry was clouded by scores of antitobacco steps taken or proposals made by citizen groups, businesses, communities, and government agencies. A small step, at first, was the decision by several hundred independent drugstores across the nation to stop selling tobacco products. Some acted under pressure from county medical societies, others under pressure from their own consciences. In drugstores that still sold cigarettes, some pharmacists sent smokers to a cash register where general merchandise was sold, refusing to ring up a tobacco sale at the pharmacy cash register. A New York State pharmacist said, "We deal in wellness. Why sell sickness?"

A spokesperson for the Tobacco Institute was not concerned, pointing out that all pharmacies combined sell only 7 percent of the cigarettes sold in the United States. Smokers turned away from drugstores "will simply walk around the corner to the nearest convenience store, grocery store, or gas station."

Nevertheless, public health advocates believed that getting tobacco sales out of drugstores was an important message to people—
that smoking is hazardous to good health. Another message about
tobacco's reputation was delivered in 1991 when the American Public Health Association joined a campaign, led by a group called the
Tobacco Divestment Project, that asked investors to get rid of their
stocks in tobacco companies. Several universities and foundations
announced that they would sell all their tobacco holdings. Several
states began considering laws that would prohibit ownership of tobacco stocks by state pension funds. Of course there was no lack of
investors who were happy to buy stocks in highly profitable tobacco
companies. Still, as the American Public Health Association stated,
it was important to champion a simple idea: "that as individuals and
as members of institutions we should not profit from tobacco addiction."

In Congress, the tobacco industry was able to block a proposed
law that would have banned smoking in virtually all buildings except private homes. In 1994, however, the Occupational Safety and
Health Administration (OSHA) proposed a rule that would ban
smoking in more than six million indoor workplaces. The rule could
not take effect until OSHA held public hearings and considered
information—pro and con—about the rule. Tobacco industry
lobbyists got busy, and in 1996 it seemed that years would pass
before OSHA put the rule into effect.

Meanwhile, all across the United States, smoking was already restricted or banned at thousands of workplaces, from small compa-

nies to industrial giants. Some companies took this step because they feared legal action by nonsmokers who were worried about the risks of passive smoking. Many firms restricted smoking because they learned that employees who smoke cost them money, by wasting time while taking smoke breaks, by taking more sick leave, and by needing more medical care from the companies' health plans. Smokers grumbled when restrictions on smoking took effect, but eventually many of them welcomed the change. Taking cigarette breaks outdoors in all kinds of weather gave them an incentive to quit. Another incentive: Some companies refuse to hire smokers, a policy that has withstood court challenges because smokers have costlier health problems. The president of an Ohio cosmetics company said, "I won't hire a smoker. Nonsmokers are healthier, have more energy, and do a better job. They make better employees."

In the mid-1990s, several new laws aimed at reducing tobacco use were proposed in the U.S. Congress. However, the tobacco industry showed that it still had the political power to delay, weaken, or kill legislation. In March 1994, for example, fifteen thousand tobacco workers were given a day off (with pay) and transportation to Washington, where they demonstrated against an increase in the federal cigarette tax. Through efforts like this and the work of well-placed tobacco-state senators and representatives, all tax proposals were quashed.

The federal tax on a pack of cigarettes remained twenty-four cents. All states and many cities and counties also have special taxes (called excise taxes) in addition to sales taxes on cigarettes and other tobacco products. Through the years, smokers have paid more and more for cigarettes, but rarely have the increases been due to taxes; tobacco companies raise prices about twice a year. Compared with other nations, the United States has one of the lowest cigarette tax rates in the world. It has failed to adjust cigarette tax rates to keep pace with inflation. Many industrialized nations impose taxes of well over two dollars a pack; in Denmark and Norway taxes are now above three dollars.

In the early 1990s, an increase of the federal tax to two dollars a pack was recommended by the American Heart Association, the American Lung Association, and the American Cancer Society. These organizations, and others promoting public health, believe that increased taxes will cause some people to quit smoking and others not to start, thereby discouraging use of the nation's number one cause of preventable death. According to one estimate, a two-dollar tax on a pack of cigarettes would reduce tobacco use by 23 percent (about seven million smokers).

Though nicotine is addictive, some people manage to give up smoking, and cost of tobacco products is known to be an incentive to quit. The bigger the tax bite, the bigger the incentive. Low-income people—and that includes most teenagers—are the ones most likely to find the cost of cigarettes prohibitive.

During the 1980s, Canada raised cigarette taxes to over three dollars a pack. Cigarette sales dropped nearly 40 percent, and smoking by teenagers was cut by about half. Then, in 1994, under pressure from the cigarette industry, Canadian lawmakers reduced the tax. The rate of teenage smoking began to rise again.

In California, a modest tax increase of an additional twenty-five

A CIGARETTE TAX BREAK

Country	Total taxes (U.S.$)	Average retail price (U.S.$)	Tax (% of retail price)
Denmark	$3.48	$4.11	85
Norway	$3.11	$4.55	68
Canada	$2.90	$4.22	69
United Kingdom	$2.85	$3.68	77
Ireland	$2.68	$3.55	75
Sweden	$2.43	$3.33	73
Finland	$2.28	$3.08	74
Germany	$2.04	$2.86	71
New Zealand	$1.93	$2.85	68
France	$1.70	$2.33	75
Belgium	$1.70	$2.31	73
Netherlands	$1.65	$2.28	72
Hong Kong	$1.50	$2.78	54
Japan	$1.21	$2.02	60
Luxembourg	$1.19	$1.76	68
Portugal	$1.17	$1.48	79
Italy	$1.16	$1.60	73
Switzerland	$1.04	$2.07	50
Argentina	$0.96	$1.37	70
Greece	$0.78	$1.13	69
Taiwan	$0.62	$1.31	47
United States	**$0.56**	**$1.89**	**30**
Korea	$0.45	$0.74	60
Spain	$0.42	$0.63	66

In 1993, the total tax on a pack of cigarettes in the United States was among the lowest in this comparison of twenty-four industrialized nations. As a percentage of the retail price, tax in the U.S. was, by far, the lowest of the twenty-four nations.

Source: Non-Smokers' Rights Association of Canada

cents a pack was approved by voters in 1988. Some of the funds were earmarked for antismoking advertisements, in print and on television, and for smoking-prevention programs. Though this tax increase didn't seem to discourage teenage smoking much, overall smoking in California dropped 28 percent in a few years. This success had its own price: With reduced sales of cigarettes, tax revenues dropped from $900 million in 1989 to less than $600 million in 1994. This also meant that the state's antismoking campaign had less money to spend.

Even though efforts to raise the federal excise tax were thwarted, the congressional debate—plus the success of California's program—led other states to raise taxes on tobacco products. Michigan and Massachusetts followed the California model, enacting new tobacco taxes with some of the funds marked for antitobacco education efforts. Part of the effort in Massachusetts—a campaign called It's Time to Make Smoking History—enlisted a corps of several hundred teenagers who were paid for part-time work. In one of their actions, a group of teenagers persuaded the only shopping mall in the city of Chicopee to declare itself smoke-free.

In 1994 the American Medical Association teamed with the Robert Wood Johnson Foundation to give financial support to antismoking groups in nineteen states, with the goal of duplicating the success of California's program in each state. The tobacco industry also swung into action in these nineteen states. In 1988 it had spent $21 million in a failed bid to block California's tax increase. Now it tried to convince state legislators that the California model was a bad idea, because increased taxes hurt poor smokers and because states only need to enforce existing laws to keep minors from buying cigarettes.

In its efforts to continue business as usual in the United States, the tobacco industry was heartened by the results of the 1994 national elections, when the Republican Party took control of the Senate and the House of Representatives. House Representative Thomas Bliley, a Republican from Virginia, became chairman of the health and environment subcommittee. Bliley has always been a champion of tobacco; Philip Morris is the biggest employer in his district. He stopped hearings that had probed the tobacco industry and said, "I don't think we need any more legislation regulating tobacco."

In 1995 and 1996 tobacco companies loosed a flood of donations to national Republican Party committees, about ten times the amount contributed to the Democratic Party. Republicans tend to be more pro-business than Democrats and often speak out against government regulation. Still, campaign donations to the Republican Party were five times greater than usual. One critic of the tobacco industry, Ann McBride of the public-interest group Common Cause, explained why: "What you have is the tobacco lobby with their backs against the wall. It is the single most aggressive campaign to use money to buy influence in Congress. It's a desperate last effort."

During his term in office, U.S. Surgeon General C. Everett Koop spoke of creating "a smoke-free society" by the year 2000 in the United States. While none of the laws or regulations proposed in the 1990s had this goal, they could nevertheless bring dramatic changes in the ways cigarettes are packaged, advertised, and sold.

Congress in 1984 had passed a law calling for four different alternating warnings to appear on cigarette packages and advertisements. Tobacco companies used their influence to ensure that the warnings would be in small print and to weaken the warnings themselves. For example, the warnings did not mention addiction or death.

Public health advocates believe that these warnings, and those on other tobacco products, are inadequate in several ways. They are small and easily overlooked. Manufacturers often print them in colors that make them difficult to read. The warnings themselves are rather vaguely worded and worn-out in an advertising sense, with the same messages being used for more than a dozen years.

At both the state and national level, groups try to persuade young people from beginning to smoke.

Laws have been proposed in Congress to toughen the messages and to word them in a more direct way. For example, the currently used warning, "Quitting Smoking Now Greatly Reduces Serious Risks to Your Health," could be replaced by "Cigarettes Kill. One in Every Three Smokers Will Die from Smoking." Equally important is making the warnings bigger and more noticeable.

In May 1995 an antismoking group called the Coalition on Smoking OR Health delivered two packs of Camel cigarettes to each member of Congress. Both packs had been manufactured in North Carolina but were strikingly different. The pack intended for the U.S. market had the usual tiny warning on its side. The other pack was to be sold in Canada and so had to comply with Canadian public health laws. The top third of the Canadian packaging was a bold warning in big letters: "Cigarettes Are Addictive."

American cigarette companies put similar warnings on packs exported to Australia. Laws in these countries require that health warnings must occupy from 30 to 40 percent of the main display area of the package. Along with the contrasting cigarette packs, the Coalition on Smoking OR Health gave each member of Congress this message: "We believe that American children are just as deserving of an honest and fair warning about the powerful addiction of tobacco as Canadian children."

Protecting the young people of the United States was the goal announced in August 1995 by President Bill Clinton when he authorized the Food and Drug Administration (FDA) to take several steps that would discourage young people from smoking. The proposed regulations included: prohibiting tobacco ads on billboards

Health warnings on cigarette packs are hard to miss in some nations but are easily overlooked on the sides of packs sold in the United States, as shown in these photos from the Coalition on Smoking OR Health.

within a thousand feet of a school, prohibiting vending-machine or mail-order sales, and prohibiting the sale or giving away of promotional items from cigarette companies. Also, only text—no pictures—would be allowed on billboards and in cigarette ads that appeared in magazines with more than 15 percent of their readership children and teenagers. Furthermore, all buyers of cigarettes would have to show a photo identification card to prove that they were eighteen years of age.

The tobacco companies immediately challenged the authority of the FDA to regulate their products. Their lawsuit was filed in North Carolina, in the heart of tobacco country, where judges have historically sided with cigarette manufacturers. Trade groups representing advertising agencies and the outdoor (billboard) advertising business also filed lawsuits in the same court. These businesses could lose many millions of dollars if this effort to protect young people from tobacco addiction was successful. Lawyers for the advertising business called the proposed regulations "an unconstitutional infringement of free speech." They predicted that the legal battle would drag on into the next century.

John Banzhaf, a lawyer who founded the antismoking group called Action on Smoking and Health (ASH), said, "We restrict advertising of drugs. If we are going to treat nicotine as a drug, then such restrictions are justified and needed."

Whether nicotine was to be considered a drug, and regulated as one, was a decision of huge importance to the tobacco industry and to the general public. Cigarette companies had always contended that people smoke for pleasure, not because they are addicted to a drug. In early 1994, FDA Commissioner Dr. David Kessler announced that it was time to consider regulating tobacco products as nicotine drug delivery systems. He said that the medical and scientific communities agreed that nicotine was addictive. "The companies are marketing a powerfully addictive agent," he said. "Despite the buzzwords used by industry, what smokers are addicted to is not 'rich aroma' or 'pleasure' or 'satisfaction.' What they are addicted to is nicotine…. To smokers who know that they are addicted, to those who have buried a loved one who was addicted, it is simply no longer credible to deny the highly addictive nature of nicotine."

Furthermore, Dr. Kessler said there was evidence that tobacco companies have long known this and may have intentionally adjusted the amounts of nicotine in cigarettes and other products to help keep their customers addicted. Some of the evidence he presented included excerpts from a company memo written in 1972 by a supervisor of research for Philip Morris: "Think of the cigarette pack as a storage container for a day's supply of nicotine…. Think of the cigarette as a dispenser for a dose unit of nicotine…. Think of a puff of smoke as the vehicle for nicotine." Dr. Kessler also quoted from a tobacco company patent: "Small doses of nicotine provide the user with certain pleasurable effects resulting in the desire for additional doses."

The FDA has further evidence, taken from tobacco company patents and other documents, that cigarette manufacturers have ways to increase or decrease the amount of nicotine, to mask the harsh taste of increased nicotine, and even to have it more concentrated in the outer half of a cigarette—the area that provides a

The chemistry of tobacco leaves has been thoroughly analyzed. Flavor and other qualities can be adjusted, but addictive nicotine is recognized as the single most important ingredient.

smoker's first few puffs. All this evidence was important because it seemed to show that tobacco companies intend their customers to be nicotine addicts. If that can be proved, then the FDA has a legal right and a responsibility to regulate tobacco products. To allow a drug on the market in the United States the FDA must find it "safe and effective." Cigarettes and other tobacco products are clearly *unsafe,* so the FDA would have the right to ban them outright.

This possibility raised all sorts of thorny issues, which Dr. Kessler acknowledged. He asked for guidance from Congress. One plan that was proposed called for the amount of nicotine to be lowered over a ten- to fifteen-year period until cigarettes were no longer addictive. This would help addicted smokers quit and help keep teenagers from starting. However, this plan would also bring health and enforcement problems. Research has already shown that smokers inhale more deeply or smoke more cigarettes in order to get the nicotine they crave. In the process they take in more tobacco poisons. Also, as nicotine levels dropped, a black market for illegal full-dose cigarettes would develop.

One bill presented in Congress in 1994 would prohibit the FDA from banning tobacco but would permit regulation of manufacturing, advertising, labeling, and sale of tobacco products. Like all other plans to regulate tobacco products, this one was strongly opposed by the tobacco industry and its allies. But the credibility of the industry was weakened by a series of documents from cigarette companies, some of which were leaked by former employees. In May 1994, for example, more than four thousand pages of documents from one tobacco company were mailed anonymously to several news organizations. The company tried to block publication of the memos, research reports, and other documents, but the California Supreme Court rejected this request.

One "strictly private and confidential" 1963 report by a high-ranking cigarette company executive stated, "We are, then, in the business of selling nicotine, an addictive drug." Other documents revealed that a researcher employed by Philip Morris in 1983 had completed a study—using rats—that showed that nicotine was addictive. A report of the study was accepted for publication by a scientific journal, but the company forced the scientist to withdraw it. Thus, the leading tobacco company knew in 1983 that nicotine was addictive, but it denied that fact in 1988 when the Surgeon General declared it. Philip Morris and the other tobacco companies continue to deny that nicotine is an addictive drug.

Other documents from tobacco company files demonstrated that they conducted secret research that showed their products caused cancer in laboratory animals. As early as 1946, twenty years before warning labels went on cigarette packs, the tobacco industry began to develop its own evidence that its products might be deadly. In 1963, executives of one company, the Brown and Williamson Tobacco Corporation, discussed whether to tell the Surgeon General what they knew about the hazards of cigarettes. They decided not to. The same company devoted a decade of research aimed at developing a "safe" cigarette. Researchers found that they couldn't remove all the harmful ingredients, so the project was dropped. Meanwhile, the tobacco industry claimed that existing cigarettes were perfectly safe.

These and other revelations eroded support for the tobacco industry in Congress. They also encouraged the growing numbers of individuals and states that were suing tobacco companies. Between 1954 and 1994 the tobacco industry was sued 813 times. Most of the cases involved a person claiming that his or her health had been harmed by tobacco. Nearly all of these lawsuits were dropped because people could not afford a long, costly legal battle with a tobacco company. Only twenty-three cases went to trial. The industry lost twice, and both losses were overturned on appeal to a higher court.

Of course the tobacco industry had the best legal teams money could buy. And proving that a product caused a person's injury or death can be difficult. Also, in an ironic twist, the tobacco industry has benefited greatly from those health warnings that it was forced to put on cigarette packs beginning in 1966. The industry's lawyers have claimed that the warning labels give notice of any hazard, so the industry can't be penalized for any harm that people claim was done by tobacco. The warning labels have acted as a powerful legal shield against smokers who have good reason to believe that their heart disease, cancers, or other illness were caused by tobacco.

Nevertheless, in the mid-1990s the tobacco industry faced a host of legal threats. The U.S. Justice Department was investigating whether cigarette companies had lied to federal regulators about the contents and ill effects of their products. The most formidable legal challenge of all was a class action suit representing forty million current smokers and fifty million former smokers filed in a New Orleans federal court. The suit was dismissed in 1996, but lawyers

representing smokers vowed to file new class action lawsuits in all fifty states. Liggett & Myers, smallest of the nation's major cigarette makers, had already settled their portion of this suit out of court. They agreed to help fund a national quit-smoking program, and to halt opposition to tougher federal regulations on tobacco. This

Executives of all the major tobacco companies have testified in congressional hearings that nicotine is not addictive.

settlement cracked the tobacco industry's previous solid front against legal challenges.

Another class action suit was brought on behalf of about sixty thousand current and former airline flight attendants. They claimed they were harmed by being exposed to secondhand smoke in airliners before smoking was banned on flights in the United States. Finally, several states sued tobacco companies on behalf of their citizens, seeking reimbursement of the health care costs of smoking. Mississippi was the first state to file such a suit, in 1994. Mississippi Attorney General Mike Moore said, "This lawsuit is premised on a simple notion: You caused the health crisis; you pay for it…. It's time these billionaire tobacco companies start paying what they rightfully owe to Mississippi taxpayers."

By mid-1996, eight other states—Connecticut, Florida, Maryland, Massachusetts, Minnesota, New Jersey, and West Virginia— had filed similar lawsuits, and others seemed likely to follow. All nine states were trying to recoup some of the public funds spent on smoking-related illness. The national cost of this illness has been estimated at $50 billion—and this may be low. Smoking accounts for at least 7 percent of all health care costs in the United States. However, some economists believe that smokers—in a perverse way—may actually *save* taxpayers money. Though they are a burden to Medicaid and other health care programs, smokers die at a younger age than nonsmokers. Then they no longer receive medical benefits or income from Social Security or pension plans.

In the courts, in state legislatures, and in Congress, the tobacco industry is under attack as never before. The medical and scientific evidence against tobacco has never been stronger; cigarettes kill more Americans than AIDS, alcohol, car accidents, murders, suicides, drugs, and fires combined. A smoke-free society may be a far-distant goal, but it is long past time for government leaders to take giant steps in that direction.

Imaginary cigarette packs, shown in a poster from the Minnesota Department of Health, feature the long-term risks and harm experienced by young smokers.

HOW TO
QUIT SMOKING—
OR NEVER START

It is difficult to find an older smoker who recommends tobacco use. Nearly all of them feel the ill effects of smoking and have tried and failed to defeat their addiction to nicotine. Still, their advice—"Don't start!"—often fails to influence teenagers. For many young people the prospect of death from lung cancer seems so far away, so unlikely, and so unimportant compared with the more immediate need to feel more grown-up and accepted by others *now.*

While it is true that the poisons in tobacco may not cause death for decades, smoking has an immediate downside. The financial cost alone can be a big turnoff, since many young people have limited funds and plenty of needs.

Also, there are social tolls that smokers pay. Since smoking is *not* the norm, with only about one out of four individuals using tobacco, a person who takes up smoking can put off people because of his or her smelly hair and breath. Smoking also begins to wear on a person's looks. "A smoker's skin never, ever has a rosy glow," said Ilona, of the Ilona of Hungary facial beauty shop on Park Avenue in New York City. "It always has a grayish or yellowish cast to it."

With forty years of experience in skin care, Ilona said she can tell immediately whether someone is a smoker. Besides color, the telltale signs include enlarged pores, breakouts, and an excess of wrinkling around the mouth. "The skin doesn't have the ability to fight any natural trauma," Ilona said. "It can take forever to heal and an eruption can linger forever." As for wrinkles around the mouth, "What would happen naturally with age is hastened a thousand times by smoking."

Despite the harmful effects known to appear soon after a person takes up smoking, many teenagers are tempted to start. Adolescence is a time of great change, a time of social pressures and often of risk-taking behavior. However, a person who reaches age eighteen without smoking usually stays a nonsmoker for life.

Consequently, in some schools students learn techniques for fighting social pressure. These include refusal skills—what to say in response to friendly or teasing pressure to start smoking—since just having some ready answers or knowing when to walk away is helpful in resisting peer pressure. They also learn how the advertisements of tobacco companies exploit the insecurities and powerful yearnings of teenagers. With the tobacco industry's $6 billion-a-year advertising and marketing campaign to make smoking look sexy, fun, and cool, more than just peer pressure is involved. The revelation that some adults are trying to lure them into a life-long addiction may help some adolescents reevaluate smoking.

Smoking just a few cigarettes should be viewed as a dangerous step toward a premature death. Nevertheless, a teenager who has not become a regular, everyday smoker has a chance to quickly halt the process of becoming addicted. Thanks to a better understanding of nicotine's effects, today even regular smokers—young and old—have more knowledge and help to overcome nicotine addiction. There are plenty of useful booklets and other materials from such groups as the American Lung Association, as well as local clinics and other support programs. (Names and addresses of helpful organizations are listed on pages 113–14.)

Some smokers turn to nicotine replacement therapy in order to quit; they stop smoking but continue to take in nicotine from gum, nasal spray, or slow-release skin patches. In 1996 nicotine gum was approved for over-the-counter sale; nicotine patches and nasal spray still require a doctor's prescription. Each of these products provides low doses of nicotine in a way that allows smokers to break their addiction slowly, over a few months, with less severe withdrawal symptoms. In the meantime the individuals benefit from not inhaling tars, carbon monoxide, and the other deadly substances in tobacco.

While nicotine patches, nasal spray, and gum have helped smokers defeat their addiction, there are no panaceas. Here is a list of general tips that have helped some people finally overcome this powerful addiction:

- Prepare. Get information about what to expect, and how to deal with withdrawal symptoms, from ex-smokers and other sources.

- Get support. Quitting with another person helps both smokers succeed, and the encouragement of friends and family—especially those who are ex-smokers—is vital.

- Really quit. Studies show that cutting down gradually is not as likely to succeed as going cold turkey, ceasing entirely.

- Keep trying. The average smoker relapses several times, most often within three months of quitting. Remember that these relapses are not failures; rather they are steps in learning how to quit. A smoker can learn from the experience, try again soon to quit, and finally succeed.

SOURCES OF HELPFUL INFORMATION

The organizations marked with an asterisk (*) have quit-smoking programs or self-help materials on how to stop. Most have free fact sheets and brochures; some charge a fee for their materials.

Action on Smoking and Health (ASH), 2013 H Street NW, Washington, DC 20006 (202-659-4310)

* American Cancer Society, 1599 Clifton Road NE, Atlanta, GA 30329 (800-227-2345)

* American Heart Association, 7272 Greenville Avenue, Dallas, TX 75231 (214-373-6300)

* American Lung Association, 1740 Broadway, New York, NY 10019 (a call to 800-LUNG-USA will connect you to the nearest American Lung Association office)

Americans for Nonsmokers' Rights, 2530 San Pablo Avenue, Suite J, Berkeley, CA 94702-2013 (510-841-3032)

Coalition on Smoking OR Health, 1150 Connecticut Avenue NW, Suite 820, Washington, DC 20036 (202-452-1184)

Environmental Protection Agency, Indoor Air Quality Information Clearinghouse, P.O. Box 37133, Washington, DC 20013-7133 (800-438-4318)

Food and Drug Administration, Office of Consumer Affairs, Room 16-85, 5600 Fishers Lane, Rockville, MD 20895 (301-443-5006)

* Hazelden, 15251 Pleasant Valley Road, P.O. Box 176, Center City, MN 55012-0176 (800-328-9000)

* The Health Connection, 55 West Oak Ridge Drive, Hagerstown, MD 21740 (800-548-8700)

* National Cancer Institute, Publication Ordering Service, 900 Rockville Pike, Bethesda, MD 20892 (800-4-CANCER)

National Center for Tobacco-Free Kids, 1707 L Street NW, Suite 800, Washington, DC 20036 (202-296-5469)

Stop Teenage Addiction to Tobacco (STAT), 511 East Columbus Avenue, Springfield, MA 01105 (413-732-7828)

GLOSSARY

addiction—the repeated use of a psychoactive (mood-altering) drug that is difficult to stop. A more complete definition of addiction—and one that certainly fits nicotine—includes the effects of the drug on the brain, a physical dependence on the drug, and a need for the drug in order to avoid unpleasant withdrawal symptoms.

cancer—a disorder in which body cells grow wildly, producing colonies called tumors, or neoplasms. Benign tumors are made up of cells similar to the surrounding tissues and are usually confined to one area. Malignant tumors are made up of cells unlike those nearby and tend to spread through the body. Cancer is the second leading cause of death in the United States today.

carbon monoxide—an odorless, dangerous gas that results when fuel is burned in an enclosed space with limited oxygen. Cigarette smoke contains carbon monoxide.

carcinogen—a substance or other factor (such as radioactivity or ultraviolet rays from sunlight) that causes cancer.

embryo—an organism in its early stages of development. During its first two months of development in its mother's womb, a human baby is called an embryo.

emphysema—labored breathing and vulnerability to infections that are a result of lung tissues being damaged by cigarette smoke or other polluted air.

epidemiology—the study of relations between disease-causing agents and communities, or populations. Much of the evidence of smoking's harm comes from epidemiological studies that compare populations of smokers with populations of nonsmokers.

fetus—an unborn human or other vertebrate that is more fully developed than an embryo. An unborn human reaches the fetus stage after two months in its mother's womb and is called a fetus until its moment of birth.

hemoglobin—a protein in the red blood cells of humans and other animals with backbones that carries vital oxygen to all parts of the body.

lobbying—trying to influence legislators and thereby the laws they produce. Sometimes lobbyists urge a legislator to propose a law or strengthen it with amendments while lobbyists representing other interests try to weaken it or persuade legislators to vote against the law.

neurotransmitter—a natural substance in the nervous system that allows the passage of certain nerve signals. The human nervous system relies on dozens of different neurotransmitters. Nicotine stimulates the release of several neurotransmitters to affect moods as well as heart rate and blood pressure.

nicotine—a complex compound from tobacco plants that serves as a chemical defense against insects. Nicotine is a powerful poison. Small doses of nicotine from dried tobacco leaves affect the human nervous system in ways that cause most tobacco users to become addicted.

pesticide—"pest killer"; a substance that kills pests. The term *biocide* (life killer) might be more appropriate, because most pesticides also kill or harm other living things.

placebo—a substance that contains no medication that is sometimes used in medical research to help learn the effects of real medication.

psychoactive—affecting the feelings or moods of a person. Nicotine is a psychoactive drug. Though its effects are less dramatic than those of illegal "hard" drugs, nicotine causes an addiction that is usually very difficult to overcome.

radioactivity—behavior of a substance in which nuclei of atoms undergo change and emit radiation in the form of alpha particles, beta particles, or gamma rays. None of this radiation can be seen or felt, but it can harm living things.

radon—a radioactive substance that is common in the soils and rocks of some areas and is one of many carcinogens in tobacco smoke.

tar—tiny particles, produced by burning tobacco, that are inhaled with tobacco smoke. Substances in tar cause cancer, and the particles also damage the lungs in other ways.

tumor—see *cancer*.

FURTHER READING

Blum, Alan, editor. *The Cigarette Underworld.* Secaucus, New Jersey: Lyle Stuart, 1985.

Centers for Disease Control and Prevention. *Preventing Tobacco Use Among Young People: A Report of the Surgeon General.* Washington, DC: U.S. Government Printing Office, 1994.

Coalition on Smoking OR Health. *Saving Lives and Raising Revenue: The Case for Major Increases in State and Federal Tobacco Taxes.* Washington, DC: Coalition on Smoking OR Health, 1993.

Ecenbarger, William. "America's New Merchants of Death." *Reader's Digest,* April 1993: 50–57.

Eckholm, Erik. "The Unnatural History of Tobacco." *Natural History,* April 1977: 22–32.

Gold, Mark. *Tobacco.* Vol. 4, *Drugs of Abuse.* New York: Plenum, 1995.

Henningfield, Jack. *Nicotine: An Old-Fashioned Addiction.* New York: Chelsea House, 1992.

"Hooked on Tobacco: The Teen Epidemic." *Consumer Reports,* March 1995: 142–47.

Klein, Richard. *Cigarettes Are Sublime.* Durham, North Carolina: Duke University Press, 1993.

Kluger, Richard. *Ashes to Ashes: America's Hundred-Year Cigarette War, the Public Health, and the Unabashed Triumph of Philip Morris.* New York: Knopf, 1996.

Krogh, David. *Smoking: The Artificial Passion.* New York: W. H. Freeman, 1991.

Lynch, Barbara, and Richard Bonnie, editors. *Growing Up Tobacco Free: Preventing Nicotine Addiction in Children and Youths.* Washington, DC: National Academy Press, 1994.

Marshall, Eliot. "Tobacco Science Wars." *Science,* April 17, 1987: 250–51.

Monroe, Judy. *Nicotine.* Springfield, New Jersey: Enslow Publishers, 1995.

Orleans, C. Tracy, and John Slade, editors. *Nicotine Addiction: Principles and Management.* New York: Oxford University Press, 1993.

Rabin, Robert, and Stephen Sugarman, editors. *Smoking Policy: Law, Politics, and Culture.* New York: Oxford University Press, 1993.

Rosenblatt, Roger. "How Do Tobacco Executives Live with Themselves?" *New York Times Magazine,* March 20, 1994: 35–41, 55, 73–75.

"Secondhand Smoke: Is It a Hazard?" *Consumer Reports,* January 1995: 27–33.

Swisher, Karin, editor. *Smoking* (At Issue: An Opposing Viewpoints Series). San Diego: Greenhaven Press, 1995.

INDEX